BREAKING THE SHACKLES OF FAMILY CURSES

"As the bird by wandering, as the swallow by flying, so the curse causeless shall not come."

Proverb 26:2

By
Franklin N. Abazie

Breaking the Shackles of Family Curses

COPYRIGHT 2018 BY Franklin N Abazie
ISBN: 978:0-9966-263-16

All right reserved. This book or any portion thereof may not be reproduced or used in any manner whatsoever without the express written permission of the publisher, except for the use of brief quotations in a book review. All Bible quotes are from King James Version and others as noted.

Published by: F N ABAZIE PUBLISHING HOUSE---a.k.a, Empowerment Bookstore:

That I may publish with the voice of thanksgiving and tell of all thy wondrous works. **Psalms26:7**

To order additional copies, wholesales or booking: Call the Church office (973-372-7518)
or Empowerment Bookstore Hotline 973-393-8518
Worship address:
343 Sanford Avenue Newark New Jersey 07106
Administrative Head Office address:
33 Schley Street Newark New Jersey 07112
Email:pastorfranknto@yahoo.com
Website www.fnabaziehealingministries.org
Publishing House: www.fnabaziepublishinghouse.org

This book is a production of F N Abazie Publishing House.

A publication Arms of Miracle of God Ministries 2018 First Edition

CONTENTS

THE MANDATE OF THE COMMISSION...........iv

ARMS OF THE COMMISSION.............................v

INTRODUCTION..viii

CHAPTER 1
1. Ancestral Pattern & Family Curses..........................20

CHAPTER 2
2. Breaking the Stronghold of Family Curses...............30

CHAPTER 3
3. Prayer of Salvation..63

CHAPTER 4
4. About the Author..69

THE MANDATE OF THE COMMISSION

"THE MOMENT IS DUE TO IMPACT YOUR WORLD THROUGH THE REVIVAL OF THE HEALING & MIRACLE MINISTRY OF JESUS CHRIST OF NAZARETH.

I AM SENDING YOU TO RESTORE HEALTH UNTO THEE AND I WILL HEAL THEE OF THY WOUNDS, SAID THE LORD OF HOST."

ARMS OF THE COMMISSION

1) F N Abazie Ministries-Miracle of God Ministries (Miracle Chapel Intl)

2) F N Abazie TV Ministries: Global Television Ministry Outreach.

3) F N Abazie Radio Ministries: Radio Broadcasting Outreach.

4) F N Abazie Publishing House: Book Publication.

5) F N Abazie Bible School: also called Word of Healing Bible School (W.O.H.B.S)

6) F N Abazie Evangelistic Ass: Miracle of God Ministries: Global Crusade

7) Empowerment Bookstore: Book distribution.

8) F N Abazie Helping Hands: Meeting the help of the needy world wide

9) F N Abazie Disaster Recovery Mission: Global Disaster Recovery.

10) F N Abazie Prison Ministry: Prison Ministry for all convicts "Second chance"

Some of our ministry arms are waiting the appointed time to commence

FAVOR CONFESSION

Father thank you for making me righteous and accepted through the blood of Jesus Christ. Because of that, I am blessed and highly favored by God. I am the subject of your affection. Your favor surrounds me as a shield, and the first thing that people see around me is your favored shield.

Thank you that I have favor with you and man today. All day long people go out of their way to bless me and help me. I have favor with everyone that I deal with today. Doors that were once closed are now opened for me. I receive preferential treatment, and I have special privileges, I am Gods favored child.

No good thing will he withhold from me. Because of Gods favor my enemies cannot triumph over my life. I have supernatural increase and promotion. I declare restoration to everything that the devil has stolen from my life. I have honor in the midst of my adversaries and an increase in assets, especially in real estate and expansion of territories.

Because I am highly favored by God, I experience great victories, supernatural turnarounds, and miraculous breakthrough in the midst of great impossibilities. I receive recognition, prominence, and honor. Petitions are granted to me even by ungodly authorities. Policies, rules, regulations, and laws are changed and reverse on my behalf.

I win battles that I don't even have to fight, because God fights them for me. This is the day, the set time and the designated moment for me to experience the free favor of God, that profusely and lavishly abound on my behalf in Jesus name. **Amen**.

DEDICATED TO LATE MR. VINCENT NNAMDI UGBEDE - a.k.a "uncle"

I dedicate this book to late Sir Vincent Nnamdi Ugbede my childhood family friend who died on August 14th 2014 in South Africa. Vincent Nnamdi Ugbede, I love you, but to God be the glory.

Although you passed away in glory to be with the Lord, the incredible memories of our youth will forever be glowing in my heart.

Although I miss you forever, I like to say thank God for the inspiration that we shared together as teenagers while you were alive. It was the shocking news of your sudden death that compelled me to write this book - *Breaking the shackles of family Curses*. This book is hereby dedicated to MR VINCENT NNAMDI YOYO UGBEDE- alias uncle. I pray to God that your soul rest in perfect peace with the Lord.

AMEN

INTRODUCTION

"As the bird by wandering, as the swallow by flying, so the curse causeless shall not come." **Proverb26:2**

I may never get the chance to meet you in person one to one, but I am glad to meet you here through the pages of this great book. I love books in print. They are the only way, the next generation can read and know more about our lives and ministry

Often people ignore the Power of curses. The truth is that, curses are real men can place a curse. Women can places curses also on people.

We were told……

"And I will bless them that bless thee, and curse him that curseth thee: and in thee shall all families of the earth be blessed." **Genesis12:3**.

"The curse of the Lord is in the house of the wicked: but he blesseth the habitation of the just." **Proverb3:33**

"And he turned back, and looked on them, and cursed them in the name of the Lord. And there came forth two she bears out of the wood, and tare forty and two children of them." **2King2:24**

By the help of God, I have complied this book to help anyone suffering from any family curse.

Therefore come with me let us unfold what the Holy Spirit is saying concerning "Breaking the shackles of family curses."

Happy Reading

HIS DESTINY WAS THE CROSS....

HIS PURPOSE WAS LOVE.....

HIS REASON WAS YOU....

"And he turned back, and looked on them, and cursed them in the name of the Lord. And there came forth two she bears out of the wood, and tare forty and two children of them."

2king2:24

"And I will bless them that bless thee, and curse him that curseth thee: and in thee shall all families of the earth be blessed."

Genesis 12:3

"The curse of the Lord is in the house of the wicked: but he blesseth the habitation of the just."

Proverb 3:33

"Thus saith the Lord; Cursed be the man that trusteth in man, and maketh flesh his arm, and whose heart departeth from the Lord.."

Jer17:5

"And the Lord God said unto the serpent, Because thou hast done this, thou art cursed above all cattle, and above every beast of the field; upon thy belly shalt thou go, and dust shalt thou eat all the days of thy life."

Genesis3:14

"Unto the woman he said, I will greatly multiply thy sorrow and thy conception; in sorrow thou shalt bring forth children; and thy desire shall be to thy husband, and he shall rule over thee."

Genesis 3:16

"And unto Adam he said, Because thou hast hearkened unto the voice of thy wife, and hast eaten of the tree, of which I commanded thee, saying, Thou shalt not eat of it: cursed is the ground for thy sake; in sorrow shalt thou eat of it all the days of thy life."

Genesis 3:17

"And Joshua adjured them at that time, saying, Cursed be the man before the Lord, that riseth up and buildeth this city Jericho: he shall lay the foundation thereof in his firstborn, and in his youngest son shall he set up the gates of it."

Joshua 6:26

"Then said he unto me, This is the curse that goeth forth over the face of the whole earth: for every one that stealeth shall be cut off as on this side according to it; and every one that sweareth shall be cut off as on that side according to it."

Zecharia5:3

CHAPTER 1
Ancestral Pattern & Family Curses

"Simeon and Levi are brethren; instruments of cruelty are in their habitation." **Genesis49:5**

As a result of our blood line, curses can travel from our great Grande' parents to our great Grande' children's children. Often Medical doctors ask blood line questions to find out the pattern in our family. Levi as a case study, had anger management problem that was never dealt with.

What did Simeon and Levi do to receive a curse of instrument of cruelty in their habitation from their father-Jacob?

"And it came to pass on the third day, when they were sore, that two of the sons of Jacob, Simeon and Levi, Dinah's brethren, took each man his sword, and came upon the city boldly, and slew all the males. And they slew Hamor and Shechem his son with the edge of the sword, and took Dinah out of Shechem's house, and went out." **Genesis 34:25-26**

The above scriptural passage reveals the incident that happened before the "Curse of anger" was pronounced upon the linage of Levi from one generation to the next, even to Moses.

Jacob their Father said....

"Simeon and Levi are brethren; instruments of cruelty are in their habitations. O my soul, come not thou into their secret; unto their assembly, mine honour, be not thou united: for in their anger they slew a man, and in their selfwill they digged down a wall. Cursed be their anger, for it was fierce; and their wrath, for it was cruel: I will divide them in Jacob, and scatter them in Israel."
(Genesis 49:5-7)

MOSES IS THE FIFTH GENERATION FROM THE TRIBE OF LEVI

"And there went a man of the house of Levi, and took to wife a daughter of Levi. And the woman conceived, and bare a son: and when she saw him that he was a goodly child, she hid him three months.

And when she could not longer hide him, she took for him an ark of bulrushes, and daubed it with slime and with pitch, and put the child therein; and she laid it in the flags by the river's brink." **(Exodus2:1-3)**

"And Pharaoh's daughter said unto her, Take this child away, and nurse it for me, and I will give thee thy wages. And the women took the child, and nursed it. And the child grew, and she brought him unto Pharaoh's daughter, and he became her son. And she called his name Moses: and she said, Because I drew him out of the water." **(Exodus2:9-10)**

The curse of anger that was not broken in the life of Simeon and Levi, was passed on to the Moses. "Any Curse" left unbroken in the family has power to rise up and prevail in the next generation. I pray you rise up in vexation to destroy any ancestral curse hanging over your life in the name of Jesus.

What are we saying?

Curses has power to travel from one generation to the next generation. Perhaps, our great Grande' parent could have brought a curse upon our life. In our case study about the life of Moses, Levi-the Grande' father brought the curse of anger into the family. Moses did not enter the Promised Land. Moses died as a result of the curse of anger. You shall not die as the result of any parental curse brought in your family by any ignorant Grande' father or mother.

For the record, most of our Grande' parents worship idols. About idols The Lord said,

"Thou shalt have no other gods before me. Thou shalt not make unto thee any graven image, or any likeness of any thing that is in heaven above, or that is in the earth beneath, or that is in the water under the earth. Thou shalt not bow down thyself to them, nor serve them: for I the Lord thy God am a jealous God, visiting the iniquity of the fathers upon the children unto the third and fourth generation of them that hate me" **(Exodus20:3-5)**

WHO CAN CURSE?

- GOD CURSES

God curse, the bible said *"And I will bless them that bless thee, and curse him that curseth thee: and in thee shall all families of the earth be blessed."* **Genesis12:3**

Our action in life can make God curse us.

We are told…

"Thou shalt have no other gods before me. Thou shalt not make unto thee any graven image, or any likeness of anything that is in heaven above, or that is in the earth beneath, or that is in the water under the earth. Thou shalt not bow down thyself to them, nor serve them: for I the LORD thy God am a jealous God, visiting the iniquity of the fathers upon the children unto the third and fourth generation of them that hate me." **Exodus20:3-5**

"Thus saith the LORD; Cursed be the man that trusteth in man, and maketh flesh his arm, and whose heart departeth from the LORD. For he shall be like the heath in the desert, and shall not see when good cometh; but shall inhabit the parched places in the wilderness, in a salt land and not inhabited." **Jer17:5**

My argument is that God curses. We must be aware of our action in life. I pray for the mercy of God to break any curse we procured from the Lord by our action in life.

Chapter 1 - Ancestral Pattern & Family Curses

"Then said he unto me, This is the curse that goeth forth over the face of the whole earth: for every one that stealeth shall be cut off as on this side according to it; and every one that sweareth shall be cut off as on that side according to it. I will bring it forth, saith the LORD of hosts, and it shall enter into the house of the thief, and into the house of him that sweareth falsely by my name: and it shall remain in the midst of his house, and shall consume it with the timber thereof and the stones thereof." **Zech5:3-5**

If any of us practice wickedness, we must repent of it and turn from our wicked ways. It takes the mercy of God to avert the curse of the Lord.

Remember......

"The curse of the LORD is in the house of the wicked:" **Proverb3:33**

- CURSE OF THE LAW

"Christ hath redeemed us from the curse of the law, being made a curse for us: for it is written, Cursed is every one that hangeth on a tree: That the blessing of Abraham might come on the Gentiles through Jesus Christ; that we might receive the promise of the Spirit through faith." **Gal3:13-14**

Jesus Christ redeemed us from this curse. It is written, *"For he hath made him to be sin for us, who knew no sin; that we might be made the righteousness of God in him."* **2cor5:21**

It takes accepting the Lord as our personal savior to be free from the curse of the Lord.

- THE CURSE OF DISOBEDIENCE

"Honor your father and mother, which is the first commandment with promise, that it may be well with you and you may live long on the earth." **Ephesians 6:2-3**

The bible says it will never be well with anyone who do not honor his parents. If you must live a curse free life, then you must honor treat and respect your parents very well in life.

- THE CURSE OF A MAN

"And Noah awoke from his wine, and knew what his younger son had done unto him. And he said, Cursed be Canaan; a servant of servants shall he be unto his brethren." **Genesis 9:24-25**

In the above passage, Noah, placed a curse on Canaan. So any man can place a curse on you, depending on the circumstance. You can attract a curse that sticks and tarries. You can also be free from usch curses, because of your righteous lifestyle.

- THE CURSE OF A PROPHET

All genuine prophets of God has the ability to curse anyone according to the laws of God. If you violate the order, you are entitled to a curse. Elisha curse forty two children. Any God ordain prophet has the warrant to decree and establish a curse on any relevant issue.

Chapter 1 - Ancestral Pattern & Family Curses

"And he turned back, and looked on them, and cursed them in the name of the Lord. And there came forth two she bears out of the wood, and tare forty and two children of them." **(2king2:24)**

Joshua the prophet placed a curse on Jericho that stayed for five hundred years. *"And Joshua adjured them at that time, saying, Cursed be the man before the LORD, that riseth up and buildeth this city Jericho: he shall lay the foundation thereof in his firstborn, and in his youngest son shall he set up the gates of it."* **Joshua6:26**.

As a prophet of God I hereby dismiss on your behave any prophetic curse placed upon your life and family in the Name of Jesus.

- THE CURSE OF BITTERNESS

"Looking diligently lest any man fail of the grace of God; lest any root of bitterness springing up trouble you, and thereby many be defiled;" **Hebrew12:15**

The curse of bitterness can destroy any family or any individual. So many of church folks have lived almost all their lives with such curses. As a prophet of God, I free you today in the Name of Jesus Christ.

How do I cure the curse of bitterness in my life?

- Peace and Holiness is the curse to the curse of bitterness

It is written, *"Follow peace with all men, and holiness, without which no man shall see the Lord:"* **Hebrew12:14**

We must embrace righteousness as a lifestyle. We must learn to forgive others of their trespasses in life. If someone violated you forgive them.

Jesus said *"For if ye forgive men their trespasses, your heavenly Father will also forgive you: But if ye forgive not men their trespasses, neither will your Father forgive your trespasses."* **Mathew6:14-15**.

As a prophet of God I hereby, destroy all root cause of bitterness in your life in the Mighty Name of Jesus.

- THE CURSE OF SEED TIME AND HARVEST

"Be not deceived; God is not mocked: for whatsoever a man soweth, that shall he also reap" **Gal6:7**

What you sow is what you will reap. *"Even as I have seen, they that plow iniquity, and sow wickedness, reap the same."* **Job4:8**

The cure for this curse is the seed you sow. If you sow good. Surely good will follow you. If you sow evil, you shall reap the same in due time. *"While the earth remaineth, seedtime and harvest, and cold and heat, and summer and winter, and day and night shall not cease."*

- THE CURSE OF SATAN

"So went Satan forth from the presence of the LORD, and smote Job with sore boils from the sole of his foot unto his crown." **Job2:7**

Satan cannot curse you, unless, you give him the room. we were told *"neither give place to the devil."*

Chapter 1 - Ancestral Pattern & Family Curses

"And he turned back, and looked on them, and cursed them in the name of the Lord. And there came forth two she bears out of the wood, and tare forty and two children of them." **(2king2:24)**

Joshua the prophet placed a curse on Jericho that stayed for five hundred years. *"And Joshua adjured them at that time, saying, Cursed be the man before the LORD, that riseth up and buildeth this city Jericho: he shall lay the foundation thereof in his firstborn, and in his youngest son shall he set up the gates of it."* **Joshua6:26**.

As a prophet of God I hereby dismiss on your behave any prophetic curse placed upon your life and family in the Name of Jesus.

- THE CURSE OF BITTERNESS

"Looking diligently lest any man fail of the grace of God; lest any root of bitterness springing up trouble you, and thereby many be defiled;" **Hebrew12:15**

The curse of bitterness can destroy any family or any individual. So many of church folks have lived almost all their lives with such curses. As a prophet of God, I free you today in the Name of Jesus Christ.

How do I cure the curse of bitterness in my life?

- Peace and Holiness is the curse to the curse of bitterness

It is written, *"Follow peace with all men, and holiness, without which no man shall see the Lord:"* **Hebrew12:14**

"He that diggeth a pit shall fall into it; and whoso breaketh an hedge, a serpent shall bite him." **Eccl 10:8**

Unless you let the devil, you are free of the curse of Satan.

CHAPTER 2
Breaking the Stronghold of Family Curses

"But Omri wrought evil in the eyes of the LORD, and did worse than all that were before him." **(1king16:25)**

"And Ahab the son of Omri did evil in the sight of the LORD above all that were before." **(1king16:30)**

"Ahaziah the son of Ahab began to reign over Israel in Samaria the seventeenth year of Jehoshaphat king of Judah, and reigned two years over Israel. And he did evil in the sight of the LORD, and walked in the way of his father, and in the way of his mother, and in the way of Jeroboam the son of Nebat, who made Israel to sin: For he served Baal, and worshipped him, and provoked to anger the LORD God of Israel, according to all that his father had done." **(1king22:51-52)**

From the above scriptural passage. The Grande' Father-Omri, to the Grande' son-Ahaziah, we noticed a stronghold of wickedness that runs in this family line. This stronghold of wickedness can destroy anyone who marry into this family blood line.

It takes a cry of faith and the mercy of God to over-power the stronghold of family curses. Every family is not the same. But the truth is there are curses that runs in most of our families.

For example in Abraham's family there was a curse on every first born.

Abraham first child was Ismael, but the blessing was on Isaac. Isaac first born was Esau, but the blessing was on Jacob. Jacob's first born was Reuben but the blessing was on Joseph.

There was a stronghold on every first born in this linage. In the same family there was a curse of barrenness. Their wives were barren at least for twenty to twenty five years each.

Sarah was barren for twenty five years, Rebecca was barren for twenty years. (See Genesis21:3-5, Genesis 25:20-21, and Genesis25:26)

- Sarah was Barren

Again in the Abrahamic family all the married women that came in to this family were barren for at least twenty to twenty five years. When Abraham married Sarah his wife she was barren for twenty five years.

"So Abram departed, as the LORD had spoken unto him; and Lot went with him: and Abram was seventy and five years old when he departed out of Haran." **Genesis12:4**

"For Sarah conceived, and bare Abraham a son in his old age, at the set time of which God had spoken to him. And Abraham called the name of his son that was born unto him, whom Sarah bare to him, Isaac. And Abraham circumcised his son Isaac being eight days old, as God had commanded him. And Abraham was an hundred years old, when his son Isaac was born unto him." **Genesis21:3-5**

Notice from the above scriptures, you will see that the curse of barrenness stayed for twenty five years in this family line.

- Rebecca was Barren

"And Isaac was forty years old when he took Rebekah to wife, the daughter of Bethuel the Syrian of Padanaram, the sister to Laban the Syrian." **Genesis25:20**

"And Isaac entreated the LORD for his wife, because she was barren: and the LORD was entreated of him, and Rebekah his wife conceived." **Genesis25:21**

"And after that came his brother out, and his hand took hold on Esau's heel; and his name was called Jacob: and Isaac was threescore years old when she bare them." **Genesis25:26**

Rachael Barren

"And when the Lord saw that Leah was hated, he opened her womb: but Rachel was barren." **Genesis29:31**

"And when Rachel saw that she bare Jacob no children, Rachel envied her sister; and said unto Jacob, Give me children, or else I die." **Genesis30:1**

There was a stronghold of lies that ran across the men and wives of this family line.

Grandmother - Sarah lied in Genesis 12:11-13.

Mother - Rebecca lied and use Jacob to steal the blessing.Genesis27:15-27

Grand-daughter - Rachael lied about her father idol which she took and hid. Genesis.31:19, verses 34 & 35.

....

Grandfather - Abraham lied Genesis12:12-13

Father - Isaac lied Genesis26:7

Grandson - Jacob lied Gensis27:19-27.

Whatsoever is the curse that runs in your own family I break it in the mighty Name of Jesus.

CURSES ARE REAL AND GODS BLESSING ARE MORE REAL!!

We are warned not to be ignorant of the devils devices. *"Lest Satan should get an advantage of us: for we are not ignorant of his devices."* **2cor2:11**

Curse are so real!! Brethren, double check on what runs in your own family. The word says *"Examine yourselves, whether ye be in the faith; prove your own selves. Know ye not your own selves, how that Jesus Christ is in you, except ye be reprobates?"*

My beloved, examine your own family carefully. If there is anything missing then we must attack it from the root. Do not take anything for granted, otherwise you will be grounded.

If your uncle could never build a house or buy a car, you must break that yoke. If you older brother could not have children, or a wife, you must break that curse. If your father died before seventy, you must break that curse. If your mother died an alcoholic, you must break that curse. If you Daddy was using drugs, you must break that curse in Jesus mighty Name.

It is the anointing of God that will make all the difference in our lives.

"And it shall come to pass in that day, that his burden shall be taken away from off thy shoulder, and his yoke from off thy neck, and the yoke shall be destroyed because of the anointing." **Isaiah10:27**

"Then Hananiah the prophet took the yoke from off the prophet Jeremiah's neck, and brake it." **Jer28:10**

I DECREE ANY CURSE UPON YOUR LIFE TO BE BROKEN IN JESUS MIGHTY NAME.

AMEN

PRAYER POINTS FOR BREAKING FAMILY CURSES

Strong yoke in my family house, hindering my breakthrough, break by fire, break by fire, break by fire, in the name of Jesus.

You family bondage, I break you today by fire, in the name of Jesus

Every power that wants me to pass through series of afflictions, be destroyed by fire, in the name of Jesus.

I separate myself from every yoke of poverty and suffering in my family line, in the name of Jesus.

I bind and cast out every spirit of delay in my life, in the name of Jesus.

Every power programming my destiny with the village people, break and lose your hold over me, in the name of Jesus.

By the sword of fire, I cut off the powers responsible for my struggles, in the name of Jesus.

My Life and destiny, you are not designed for stagnation and limitation, in the name of Jesus.

Ancestral chains binding me and my family together, break by fire, in the name of Jesus.

O God arise and purge my foundation, in the name of Jesus.

Chapter 2 - Breaking the Stronghold of Family Curses

Blood of Jesus, deliver me from this family bondage, in the name of Jesus.

You powers that has buried my names beside a rat in the spirit realm, receive the fire of hypertension and die, in Jesus name.

Glory robbers in my father's house, stealing from the garden of my destiny, die by fire, in the name of Jesus.

I jump out from every family cage, by the power in the blood of Jesus.

O God arise and make me re-write my family history, in the name of Jesus.

Every evil pattern of failure and poverty operating in my family-line, we loose and separate from you in the name of Jesus.

Every spirit of polygamous witchcraft rising on my horses, I pull you down by fire, in the name of Jesus.

Every ancestral power that wants me to stay older in my parents' house, I reject that curse, in the name of Jesus.

The anointing of near success syndrome in my life, be arrested by fire, in the name of Jesus.

Every dream of poverty to my village, be destroyed by fire, in Jesus name.

My Father, let your power capture and dismantle any wicked spirit that is sitting on the glory of my family, in the name of Jesus.

Evil veil covering the glory of my family, be destroyed by fire, in Jesus name.

Every wind of lack blown to me by the wicked, I blow you back by fire, in the name of Jesus.

Collective family bondage in my foundation, break and release me, in Jesus name.

Every generational struggles and poverty my family is known for, be destroyed by fire, in Jesus name.

You idol tree where my family life and foundation is tied and covenanted in the name of Jesus Christ wither and dry up.

Every evil my family have done in the past, which have mortgaged the family's wealth to demonic powers, be destroyed now by the blood of Jesus Christ.

Holy Ghost fire burn all the shrines in my foundation and family in Jesus name.

Every destructive spirit of anger and late marriage in my foundation and family be destroyed by the blood of Jesus Christ.

Every evil power that have the history of my family and foundation in the name of Jesus Christ I bind you and cast you into the lake of fire.

Every generational strongman of my foundation and family be bind and be cast into the lake of darkness in Jesus name.

Every custom of people holding me captive in the name of Jesus Christ be destroyed in the name of Jesus Christ.

Ancestral evil link transmission from my foundation, I break and disconnect you today by the blood of Jesus.

Let the anointing of the Holy Spirit break every yoke of backwardness and begging, in the name of Jesus.

Evil idols in my father's side demanding for worship, catch fire, in the name of Jesus.

Powers using my family name to attack us, run mad, and die, in Jesus name.

Whatever evil that is currently being programmed into my foundation, I exhume you by the Holy Ghost fire, in Jesus name I shall not labor in vain I claim my total deliverance from family bondage, in the name of Jesus.

By the blood of Jesus, I recover whatever the enemy has stolen from me in the past, present and my future, in the name of Jesus.

Prayer Point for Protection

- It is written; do not be afraid of sudden terror; nor of the trouble from the wicked when it comes; for the Lord will be your confidence. And will keep your foot from being caught (Proverb 3:26).

- Therefore, O Lord, cover us and our loved ones from the activities of terrorists, in Jesus name!

- It is written; avenge me of my adversary (Luke. 18:3).

- Therefore, O Lord, arise and avenge us of all my adversaries in the name of Jesus!

- It is written; they fought from the heavens; the stars from their courses fought against Sisera (Judges. 5:20).

- Therefore O heavens, fight for us in Jesus name!

- It is written; I will purge the rebels from among you, and those who transgress against Me; I will bring them out of the country where they dwell, but they shall not enter the land of Israel. They will know that I am the Lord (Ezekiel. 20:38)

- Therefore, O Lord, purge and sanitize our household in the name of Jesus!

- It is written; then it was so, after all your wickedness – "woe, woe to you!" says the Lord God (Ezekiel. 16:23)

Chapter 2 - Breaking the Stronghold of Family Curses

- Therefore, woe unto all the vessels that the enemy is using to do us harm in the name of Jesus!

- It is written; behold therefore, I stretch out my hand against you, admonished your allotment, and gave you up to the will of those who hate you... (Ezek. 16:27)

- Therefore, let our enemies be delivered into the hands of their enemies in Jesus name!

- It is written; you shall be for fuel of fire; your blood shall be in the midst of the land. You shall not be remembered, for I the Lord have spoken (Ezekiel. 21:32)

- Therefore, let all our spiritual enemies become fuel for divine fire in Jesus name!

- It is written; then they will know that I am the Lord, when I have set a fire in Egypt and all her helpers are destroyed (Ezekiel. 30:8).

- Therefore, O Lord, let all the helpers of our enemies be destroyed in the name of Jesus.

- It is written; and the people to whom they prophesy shall be cast out in the streets of Jerusalem because of the famine and the sword; they will have no one to bury them – them nor their wives, their sons nor their daughters – for I will pour their wickedness on them (Jer. 14:16).

- Therefore, O Lord, pour the wickedness of those who seek to destroy us upon their own heads in the name of Jesus!

- It is written; call together the archers against Babylon. All you who bend the bow encamp against it all around; let none of them escape. Repay her according to her work; According to all she has done, do to her; for she has been poured against the Lord, against the Holy one of Israel (Jer. 50:29).

- Therefore, let all the hosts of the Lord turn against our spiritual enemies in Jesus name!

- It is written; let God arise, let His enemies be scattered; let those also who hate him flee before him (Psalms. 68:1).

- Therefore, O God, arise and let all your enemies in our lives be scattered in Jesus name!

- It is written; and He that searches the hearts knows what the mind of the spirit is, because He makes intercession for the saints according to the will of God (Romans 8:27)

- Therefore, the intercessory prayers of Jesus, who is seated on the right hand of the throne of God, will not be in vain over our lives, in the name of Jesus.

- It is written; the Lord is your keeper; the Lord is the shade at your right hand. The sun shall not strike you by day, nor the moon by night. The Lord shall preserve you from all evil; He shall preserve your soul. The Lord shall preserve your going out and your coming in from this time forth, and even forevermore (Psalms. 121:5-8)

- Therefore, O Lord, spread your covering of fire and the blood of Jesus over us and our loved ones, in the name of Jesus.

Chapter 2 - Breaking the Stronghold of Family Curses

- It is written; rejoice always, pray without ceasing, in everything give thanks; for this is the will of God in Christ Jesus for you (1 Thess. 5:16:18).

- Therefore, we thank you Father, for raising a spiritual shield over our loved ones and us. Thank you for giving us the heart for appreciating everything you are doing for us. Thank you for filling our hearts and our home with joy and peace that surpasses all understanding. Blessed be your name for all the answers to our prayers in the name of Jesus!

- You are holy, holy, Lord God Almighty, who was and is and is to come, Amen!

- O Lord, let our season of divine intervention appear in the name of Jesus!

- O you gates in the heavenlies standing against our destiny, lift up your heads in the name of Jesus!

- O you gates in the waters standing against our destiny, lift up your heads in the name of Jesus!

- O you gates in the earth standing against our destiny, lift up your heads in the name of Jesus!

- O you gates under the earth standing against our destiny, lift up your heads in the name of Jesus!

- O God, arise and destroy every gate keeper assigned against our lives in the name of Jesus!

- We break the backbone of every spirit of scarcity in our lives in the name of Jesus!

- O Lord anoint our eyes to see divine opportunities in the name of Jesus!

- Lord let every blindness to the treasures of our lives be cleared in the name of Jesus!

- Let our divine helpers appear in the name of Jesus!

- We declare, O Lord, that the rest of our lives will be better than the first part, in Jesus name!

- We declare, O Lord that will overcome obstacles and defeat every enemy, in Jesus name!

- We declare, O Lord that every blessing and promise that you put in our hearts will come to pass because this is our time for favor, in Jesus name!

- We declare, O Lord that this is a new season of increase in our lives. We speak health, wisdom, creativity, divine connections, and supernatural opportunities. They are coming our way, in Jesus name!

- We declare, O Lord that we choose faith over fear. We are victorious in faith, in Jesus name!

- We declare, O Lord that that we are not just surviving, this is our time to thrive in prosperity, in Jesus name!

- We declare, O Lord that we will believe that we have received in the spirit even though we do not see anything happening in the flesh, in Jesus name!

- We declare, O Lord that our rewards are being transferred to us because we remain in faith, in Jesus name!

- We declare, O Lord that doubt will not ruin our optimistic spirit, in Jesus name!

- We declare, O Lord that we are prisoners of hope and get up every morning expecting your favor, in Jesus name!

- We declare, O Lord that you will do amazing things in our lives, in Jesus name!

- We declare, O Lord that we are closer to your abundant blessing than we think, our time has come, your promises will come to pass, in Jesus name!

- We declare, O Lord that we will stay in an attitude of faith and expectation, in Jesus name!

- We declare, O Lord that we are not worried, we know that you are our vindicator. It may seem to be taking a long time, but we will reap in due season if trust in you Lord, in Jesus name!

- We declare, O Lord that you know the secret petitions our heart and we believe that they will come to fulfilment, in Jesus name!

- We declare, O Lord that you will open new doors for us, in Jesus name!

- We declare, O Lord that we will see your goodness, in Jesus name!

- We declare, O Lord that this is our time to believe because favour is coming our way, in Jesus name!

- We declare, O Lord that you have paved the way to abundant prosperity for us, prosperity more than we can every dream of or imagine, for your sake, in Jesus name!

- We declare, O Lord that in your eyes our future is extremely bright, in Jesus name!

- We declare, O Lord that we will rise higher and higher and see more of your favour and blessings and we will live the prosperous life you have in store for us, in Jesus name!

- We declare, O Lord that we may have a lot of turmoil, but we know that everything is going to be alright, in Jesus name!

- We declare, O Lord that we have faith because we have put you first, in Jesus name!

- We thank you, O Lord that our set time for favour is here, in Jesus name!

- We declare, O Lord that our hour of deliverance has come, in Jesus name!

- We declare, O Lord that there is no limit to what we can do, in Jesus name!

- We declare, O Lord that there is no obstacle we cannot overcome, in Jesus name!

Chapter 2 - Breaking the Stronghold of Family Curses

- We declare, O Lord that that we have seen your accomplishments and they are good, in Jesus name!

- We declare, O Lord that there is no challenge that is too great for us because you are with us, in Jesus name!

- We declare, O Lord that you always succeed, in Jesus name!

- We declare, O Lord that there is no financial difficulty or situation in our lives that is too great for you to resolve, in Jesus name!

- We declare, O Lord that you are our Father Jehovah Jireh and that you own everything and you are our provider, in Jesus name!

- We declare, O Lord that your promises declare that we are destined to live a victorious life, in Jesus name!

- We declare, O Lord that we are your children, in Jesus name!

- We declare, O Lord that the seeds of increase, success, and promotion are taking a new root; your favour will spring forth in our lives in a great way; we will see new seasons of blessings and new seasons of your favour. It's our time to have abundant faith, in Jesus name!

- O Lord, it is written; according to your faith, it will be done unto you. Ps. 2:8 says *"ask me and I will give you the nations as your inheritance."*

- Therefore, we ask you Lord to fulfil our highest hopes and dreams, in Jesus name!

- We ask you this day, O Lord to give us our abundant blessing now, in Jesus name!

- We dare to exercise our faith by asking you O Lord so that we may receive indeed, in Jesus name!

- We thank you O Lord that for encouraging our faith, in Jesus name!

- We declare, O Lord that this is our time for favour, in Jesus name!

- We declare, O Lord that this is our time to prosper abundantly, in Jesus name!

- We declare, O Lord that this is our time to have instant answers to prayer, in Jesus name!

- We declare, O Lord that this is our time to ask and receive, in Jesus name!

- We declare, O Lord that this is our time to thank you and testify for answered prayer, in Jesus name!

- We declare, O Lord that we are blessed and that goodness and mercy are following us right now, in Jesus name!

- We declare, O Lord that you favour is surrounding us like a shield – you prosper us even in the desert, in Jesus name!

- We declare, O Lord that you have great things for us in the spirit and that you have already released favour into our prayers, in Jesus name!

Chapter 2 - Breaking the Stronghold of Family Curses

- We declare, O Lord that you are a great and Holy God, in Jesus name!

- It is written; delight yourself in the Lord and he will give you the desires of your heart (Ps 37:4).

- We therefore declare, O Lord that we delight in you because you are our Father God and because we are your children you have made us the head and not the tail. You want to take us to a new level of prosperity, in Jesus name!

- We declare, O Lord that because we are your children, we are more than conquerors, in Jesus name!

- We declare, O Lord that we are blessed and you supply all our needs. We have more than enough, in Jesus name!

- We declare, O Lord that we have abundant favour indeed, in Jesus name!

- We declare, O Lord that we are filled indeed with the presence of the Holy Spirit, in Jesus name!

- We declare, O Lord that we have abundant faith indeed, in Jesus name!

- We declare, O Lord that you have answered our prayers, in Jesus name!

- We declare, O Lord that our debts are all paid up, in Jesus name!

- We declare, O Lord that we are healthy, in Jesus name!

- We declare, O Lord that we have no lack and that we have more than enough, in Jesus name!

- We declare, O Lord that we are extremely blessed so much that we can bless your kingdom, in Jesus name!

- We declare, O Lord that we are extremely blessed so much that we can bless others, in Jesus name!

- We declare, O Lord that we have entered into an anointing of ease, in Jesus name!

- We declare, O Lord that for every opportunity we have missed, every chance we've blown, you will turn the clock and bring bigger and better things across our path , in Jesus name!

- We declare, O Lord that we will not settle for less than your best, in Jesus name!

- Please restore the time that we have lost, O Lord that, in Jesus name!

- Restore our victories, O Lord, in Jesus name!

- Restore our lost joy, lost peace, lost health, lost insight, lost faith, lost dedication and desire to please you, we declare, O Lord in Jesus name!

- We declare, O Lord that you use what was meant for our harm to our advantage, in Jesus name!

- We declare, O Lord that you are a faithful God, in Jesus name!

Chapter 2 - Breaking the Stronghold of Family Curses

- We declare, O Lord that you will blossom our lives in ways that we can never imagine, in Jesus name!

- We know, O Lord that you will bless us abundantly, in Jesus name!

- We know, O Lord that you will provide divine connections, in Jesus name!

- We declare, O Lord that we are not suffering – we are blessed, in Jesus name!

- We declare, O Lord that our difficulties will give way to new growth, new opportunities, and new vision, in Jesus name!

- O Lord let us see your blessing bloom in our lives in ways we would never dreamt possible, in Jesus name!

- We declare, O Lord that we will stay in faith, so that what was meant to stop us will not be a stumbling block but a stepping stone taking us to a higher level, in Jesus name!

- We declare, O Lord that we are not ordinary, but we are children of the most high God, in Jesus name!

- We declare, O Lord that we created to rise above problems, in Jesus name!

- We declare victory over strife O Lord, in Jesus name!

- We declare, O Lord that no weapon formed against us shall prosper, in Jesus name!

- We declare, O Lord that we are healthy and that no sickness shall live in us, in Jesus name!

- We declare, O Lord that triumph is our birthright, in Jesus name!

- We declare, O Lord that our setbacks are simply setups for greater comebacks that will place us to be better than we were before, in Jesus name!

- We declare, O Lord that with you all things are possible, in Jesus name!

- We declare, O Lord that we are in agreement with you. We know you have supernatural favour in store for us. You have supernatural opportunities, supernatural healing and supernatural restoration, in Jesus name!

- We declare, O Lord that you want to do unusual things in our lives, in Jesus name!

- We declare, O Lord that in faith, we have expectation deep in our spirits, in Jesus name!

- We declare, O Lord that this will not be a survival year but a supernatural year in which you will abundantly come through for us, in Jesus name!

- We believe, O Lord that you have come through for us, in Jesus name!

- We declare, O Lord that because we hope in you, we will not be put to shame, in Jesus name!

- We declare, O Lord that your word is right and true, you are faithful in all you do, in Jesus name!

Chapter 2 - Breaking the Stronghold of Family Curses

- We declare, O Lord that you are our refuge and strength, an ever present helper, in Jesus name!

- We declare, O Lord that we will cast our cares on you and you will sustain us, you will never let the righteous fall, in Jesus name!

- We declare, O Lord that you are the strength of our hearts and our portion forever, in Jesus name!

- We declare, O Lord that you are our dwelling, therefore, no harm will befall us and no disaster will come near our tent, in Jesus name!

- We declare, O Lord that you are our refuge and our fortress, in Jesus name!

- We declare, O Lord that you will command your angels concerning us to guard us in all our ways, in Jesus name!

- We declare, O Lord that even in darkness the light will dawn for us, in Jesus name!

- We declare, O Lord that your word is eternal and stands firm in the heavens, in Jesus name!

- We declare, O Lord that your faithfulness will continue throughout all generations, in Jesus name!

- We declare, O Lord that you will keep us from harm; you will watch over our lives; you will watch over our coming and our going both now and for evermore, in Jesus name! (Ps. 121)

- Thank you O Lord for the assurance that you are watching over us even when we sleep, in Jesus name! (Ps. 13:5-6)

- We declare, O Lord that you will drive those that do evil away from us and that you will protect us from their influence, in Jesus name! (Ps. 66:1-4)

- We will shout with joy to you O Lord, we will sing the glory of your name and make your praise glorious. How awesome are your deeds! So great is your power that your enemies cringe before you, in Jesus name!

- We declare, O Lord that that we will give you thanks for you answered us, in Jesus name! (Ps. 118:21)

- We declare, O Lord that we will praise you with all our hearts; before the gods we will sing your praise. We will bow down towards your Holy temple and will praise your name for your love and your faithfulness, for you have exalted above all things, your name and your word, in Jesus name! (Ps. 138:1-3)

Amen!

Chapter 2 - Breaking the Stronghold of Family Curses

CONCLUSION

"And I will bless them that bless thee, and curse him that curseth thee: and in thee shall all families of the earth be blessed." **Genesis12:3**

All I have said from the beginning of this book to this page, will not make any sense if you have not given your life to Jesus Christ.

"Therefore if any man be in Christ, he is a new creature: old things are passed away; behold, all things are become new." **2cor5:17**

Now repeat this Prayer after me

Say Lord Jesus, I accept you today, as my Lord and my savior, forgive me of my sins wash me with your blood. Right now, I believe, I am sanctified, I am save, I am free, I am free from the Power of sin to serve the Lord Jesus. Thank you Lord for saving me. Amen.

What must I do to determine my divine visitation?

To determine divine visitation you must be born again. The word says as many as received him, to them gave He power to become the sons of God. Even to them that believe on his name.

To qualify for divine visitation do the following sincerely,

1) Acknowledge that you are a sinner and that He died for you. **Rom3:23**.

2) Repent of your sins. **Acts 3:19, Luke13:5, 2Peter3:9**

3) Believe in your heart that Jesus died for your sin. **Romans10:10**

4) Confess Jesus as the Lord over your life. **Romans10:10, Acts2:21**

I will strongly recommend that you become an active member of this prayer ministry.

Chapter 2 - Breaking the Stronghold of Family Curses

WISDOM KEYS

Every Productive Society is a society heading to the top

Millions of Nigerians run away from Nigeria, very few Nigerians stay in Nigeria.

My decision to return Nigeria is the will of God for my life

My short coming in America after 18 years, trained me to be wise, to think, reflect and reason appropriately.

If you train your mind to reason it will train your hands to earn money.

It is absurd to use the money of the heathen to build the kingdom of the living God.

Every Ministry reveals its agenda and goal either at the beginning or at the end. Be careful of your life it is your first Ministry.

The average American mind is conditioned for a continual quest to get new things and (discard the former) and throw away old things.

When I considered well, my BMW jeep became my initial deposit for the work of the ministry in Nigeria

Everyone is waiting for you to change your mind until you change your thinking nothing changes around you.

Multiple academic degrees in other discipline gave me the chance to think, reflect and reason

What so everyone are thinking and reflecting at the moment reveals you to the time and the now factor

All events and intents are the product of precise thought processes, accurate reason every event is designed for a designated timeline

Wisdom is your ability to think, to create and invent. If you can think wise enough you will come out of penury

The distance between you and success is your creative ability to think reason and reflect accurate.

Success is the result of hard work, commitment resolve and determination learning from past mistakes and failing.

If you organize your mind you have organized your life and destiny.

There is a thin line between success and failure. If you look above and beyond you are on your way to success.

Wealth is your ability to think, power is your ability to reason and success is your ability to be informed.

If you can make use of your mind by thinking and reasoning God will make use of your life and destiny.

Think and Be Great

Reflect, Reason, think and be great

That you will make it is your intention; that you will survive is your resolve, that you will succeed with changes is your determination, personal efforts and hard work.

No man was born a failure. Lack of vision is the end product of failure.

Working with mental patients encourages and aspire me to be a productive observant and dedicated to my assignment.

Successful people are not magicians, it is the will power combined with hard work, and determination and a resolve to succeed that make them succeed.

In the unequivocal state of the mind, intention is not a location or a position it is the state of the mind.

So many people think that they think. The mind is used to think reflect and reason. You will remain blind with your eye open until you can see with your mind by thinking.

There is no favoritism in accurate and precise calculation

Although knowledge is power, information is the key and gateway to a great future.

It will take the hand of God to move the hand of man.

With the backing of the great wise God, nothing will disconnect you from your inheritance.

As long as you have wisdom and understanding of God, Satan and evil cannot manipulate your life and destiny.

You have come this far by yourself judgment and decision you have made in the past, now lean and listen to God for another dimension of greatness.

Great people are common people it is extra ordinary effort and the price of sacrifice that produces greatness.

As a mental direct care worker I saw a great pastor and a motivational speaker within myself.

Menial job does not reduce your self-worth, until you resolve to achieve greatness see greatness in all you do; you will never count in your community

The principle of Jesus will solve your gambling and addiction problems

The man of Jesus will lead you into heaven,

Everyone have their self-appraisal and what they think about you. Until you discover yourself other opinion about you will alter the real you.

Supervisors and directors are just a position in the chain of command in a work place. Never allow your supervisor hierarchy to alter your opinion about yourself.

Everyone can come out of debt if they make up their mind.

That I am not a decision maker at work does not diminish my contribution to my world.

Although it appears like it was a poor decision to accept a direct care employment at a psychiatric hospital as I reflect of my nine years of experience, it became apparent that I have learnt and experienced enough for my next assignment.

Chapter 2 - Breaking the Stronghold of Family Curses

Self-encouragement and determination is a resolve of the heart.

If you are determined to make a difference, and do the things that make a difference you will eventually make a difference.

Good things do not come easy

Short cuts will cut your life short.

Those who look ahead move ahead.

Life is all about making an impact. In your life time strive to make an impact in your community.

Make friends and connect with people who are moving ahead of you in life.

If you can look around well you have come a long way in your life, made a lot of difference and realized a lot of success in life.

If you are my old friend, hurry up to reach out to me before I become a stranger to you.

Everything I am blessed with inspirations from God, that change my definition and interpretation of the world around me.

I thought I was stagnant and lonely until I looked around and noticed my children running around and my wife cooking.

At 40 I resigned my Job to seek the Lord forever.

My ministry took a drastic rise to the top when the wisdom of God visited me with knowledge and understanding.

You will be a better person if you understand the characteristics of your personality – your mood swings attitudes and habits.

It is the seed of love you sow into the heart of a child and a woman that you reap in due time.

Love is not selfish, love share everything including the concealed secrets of the mind.

As long as you have a prayer life and a bible; you will never feel lonely, rejected and idle in the race of life.

When good friends disconnect from you, let them go, they might have seen something new in a different direction.

Confidence in yourself and in God is the only way to bring you out of captivity

Never train a child to waste his/her time.

The mind is the greatest assets of a great future.

You walk by common sense run by principles and fly by instruction.

Those who fly in flight of life fly alone.

Up in the air you are alone. No one can toll you accept the compass of knowledge and information

I have seen a tolling vehicle I have seen a tolling ship I have never seen a tolling airplane.

I exercise my judgment and make a decision every minute of the day.

Decisions are crucial, critical and vital with reference to your future.

So many people wish for a great future. You can only work towards a great future.

Your celebrity status began when you discovered your talent. What are you good at? Work at it with all commitment.

Prayers will sustain you but the wisdom of God will prosper you.

When I met Oyedepo, his teachings changed my perspective, but when I met Ibiyeomie; His teaching changed my perception.

I will be successful in ministry if only I concentrate and focus my energy in the work of the ministry.

It took the late Dr. Vincent Pearle Norman's book to open my mind towards kingdom success.

CHAPTER 3
PRAYER OF SALVATION

"Neither is there salvation in any other: for there is none other name under heaven given among men, whereby we must be saved." **Acts4:12**

The purpose of this book is for us to receive genuine salvation. If you have read all through this book without a decision for Jesus Christ, then the purpose has been defeated.

Salvation means deliverance from sin and evil forces of destruction. It is my prayer that you embrace the Lord today. We are excited as a prayer family to hear of your testimony.

"Now when they heard this, they were pricked in their heart, and said unto Peter and to the rest of the apostles, Men and brethren, what shall we do? Then Peter said unto them, Repent, and be baptized every one of you in the name of Jesus Christ for the remission of sins, and ye shall receive the gift of the Holy Ghost." Acts2:37-38

"And they said, Believe on the Lord Jesus Christ, and thou shalt be saved, and thy house." **Acts16:30**.

It is my prayer for you to make a decision today for Jesus Christ. Join a bible believing church or you can join us. We prayer online every Monday and Wednesday 9:00pm to 10:00pm 515-739-1216 code 162288.

You can worship with us,

MIRACLE OF GOD MINISTRIES

343 Sanford Avenue, Newark NJ 07106

Wednesdays-Bible study-7pm-9pm,

Fridays 10:45pm-1am Encounter night,

Sundays 10:45am-12:45pm anointing service.

MIRACLE CARE OUTREACH

"...But that the members should have the same care one for another" **1cor12:25**

We are all members of the body of Christ. Jesus commanded us to love our neighbor as ourselves. This includes caring for one another as a member of one body. True love is expressed in caring and giving. The word says for God so Love He gave....

Reach out to someone in need of Jesus, help someone in crisis find Christ. Look out and prove your love to Jesus by caring and inviting your friends and associates to find Jesus the Healer.

Invite your friends to our Home Care Cell Fellowship (Miracle chapel Intl Satellite fellowship) In the USA at 33 Schley Street Newark New Jersey 07112.

If you are in Nigeria—**MIRACLE OF GOD MINISTRIES**

A.K.A"MIRACLE CHAPEL INTL" Mpama – Egbu-Owerri Imo state Nigeria.

Chapter 3 - Prayer of Salvation

(Home Care Cell fellowship Group). We meet every Tuesday at 6:00pm-7:00pm.

LIFE IS NOT ALL ABOUT DURATION BUT ITS ALL ABOUT DONATION

What does the above statement mean?....

"Life consists not in accumulation of material wealth.." **Luke12:15.**

"But it's all about liberality....meaning- what you can give and share with others." **Proverb11:25.**

When you live for others--You live forever- because you out live your generation by the legacy you live behind after you depart into glory to be with the Lord. But when you live to yourself - you are reduced to self—you are easily forgotten when you die and depart in glory.

Permit me to admonish you today to live your life to be a blessing to a soul connected to you today.

I want you to know that so many souls are connected and looking up to you, and through you so many souls will be saved and rescued from destruction. Will you disciple someone today to find Jesus Christ?

"As a genuine Christian; it is your duty to evangelize Jesus Christ to all you meet on your way. Jesus is still in the healing business-Jesus is still doing miracles from time of old to now.

Therefore tell someone about Jesus Christ today, disciple and bring them to Church."

John 1:45 Philip findeth Nathanael....

Please to prove the sincerity of your love for God today; please become a soul winner. The dignity of your Christianity is hidden in your boldness to proclaim and evangelize Jesus Christ to all you meet on your way.

There is a question mark on the integrity of your Christianity until you become a life soul winner. Invite someone to join us worship the Lord Jesus this coming Sunday.

MIRACLE OF GOD MINISTRIES

PILLARS OF THE COMMISSION

We Believe Preach and Practice the following,

1) We believe and preach Salvation to every living human being

2) We believe and preach Repentance and forgiveness of sins

3) We believe and preach the baptism of the Holy Spirit and Spiritual gifts

4) We believe and teach the Prosperity

5) We believe and preach Divine Healing and Miracles (Signs & Wonder)

6) We believe and preach Faith

7) We believe and Proclaim the Power of God (Supernatural)

8) We believe and Proclaim Praise& Worship to God

9) We believe and preach Wisdom

10) We believe and preach Holiness (Consecration)

11) We believe and preach Vision

12) We believe and teach the Word of God

13) We believe and teach Success

14) We believe and practice Prayer

15) We believe and teach Deliverance

This 15 stones form the Pillars of Our Commission.

Become part of this church family and follow this great move of God.

MY HEART FELT PRAYER FOR YOU

It is my desire for you to encounter the Lord Jesus Christ. Seek Him in truth and you shall find rest for your soul.

Now let me Pray for you:

Father I thank you for giving me the spirit of endurance. Lord God of heaven grant me the courage and the fortitude to survive any prevailing obstacle ragging against my life and destiny. I give you thanks in advance. In Jesus Mighty Name.

Amen.

CHAPTER 4
ABOUT THE AUTHOR

Rev Franklin N Abazie is the founding and Presiding Pastor of Miracle of God Ministries with headquarters in Newark, New Jersey USA and a branch church in Owerri- Imo State Nigeria. He is following the footsteps of one of his mentors, Oral Roberts (Healing Evangelist) of the blessed memory.

The Lord passed Oral Roberts healing mantle two days before he went to be with the Lord at age 91 into the hand of healing evangelist-Rev Franklin N Abazie in a vision.

In all his services the Power and Presence of God is present to heal all in his audience. He is an ordained man of God with a Healing Ministry reviving the healing and miracle ministry of Jesus Christ of Nazareth.

Pastor Franklin N Abazie, is called by God with a unique mandate:

"THE MOMENT IS DUE TO IMPACT YOUR WORLD THROUGH THE REVIVAL OF THE HEALING & MIRACLE MINISTRY OF JESUS CHRIST OF NAZARETH.

I AM SENDING YOU TO RESTORE HEALTH UNTO THEE AND I WILL HEAL THEE OF THY WOUNDS. SAID THE LORD OF HOST"

He is a gifted ardent Teacher of the word of God who operates also in the office of a Prophet, generating and attracting undeniable signs & wonders, special miracles and healings, with apostolic fireworks of the Holy Ghost.

He is the founding and presiding senior Pastor of this fast growing Healing ministry.

He has written over 86 inspirational, healing and transforming books covering almost all aspect of divine healing and life. He is happily married and blessed with children.

BOOKS BY REV FRANKLIN N ABAZIE

1) Commanding Abundance
2) The outcome of faith
3) Understanding the secret of prevailing prayers
4) Understanding the secret of the man God uses
5) Activating my due Season
6) Overcoming Divine Verdicts
7) The Outcome of Divine Wisdom
8) Understanding God's Restoration Mandate
9) Walking in the Victory and Authority of the truth
10) Gods Covenant Exemption
11) Destiny Restoration Pillars
12) Provoking Acceptable Praise
13) Understanding Divine Judgment
14) Activating Angelic Re-enforcement
15) Provoking Un-Merited Favor
16) The Benefits of the Speaking faith
17) Understanding Divine Arrangement
18) Understanding Divine Healing
19) The Mystery of Endurance
20) Obeying Divine Instructions
21) Understanding the Voice of God
22) Never give up on Hope
23) The prevailing Power of faith
24) Understanding Divine Prosperity

25) The Reward of Prayer
26) Covenant Keys to Answered Prayers
27) Activating the Forces of Vengeance
28) Put your faith to work
29) Where is your trust?
30) The Audacity of the Blood of Jesus
31) Redeeming Your Days
32) The force of Vision
33) Breaking the shackles of Family Curses
34) Wisdom for Marriage Stability
35) Overcoming prevailing challenges
36) The Prayer solution
37) The power of Prayer
38) The Effective Strategy of Prayer
39) The prayer that works
40) Walking in Forgiveness
41) The power of the grace of God
42) The Power of Persistence
43) Overcoming Divine verdicts
44) The audacity of the blood of Jesus.
45) The prevailing power of the blood of Jesus
46) The benefit of the speaking faith.
47) Fearless faith
48) Redeeming Your Days.
49) The Supernatural Power of Prophecy
50) The companionship of the Holy Spirit
51) Understanding Divine Judgement

52) Understanding Divine Prosperity
53) Dominating Controlling Forces
54) The winners Faith
55) Destiny Restoration Pillars
56) Developing Spiritual Muscles
57) Inexplicable faith
58) The lifestyle of Prayer
59) Developing a positive attitude in life.
60) The mystery of Divine supply
61) Encounter with the Power of God
62) Walking in love
63) Praying in the Spirit
64) How to provoke your testimony
65) Walking in the reality of the Anointing
66) The reality of new birth
67) The price of freedom
68) The Supernatural power of faith
69) The intellectual components of Redemption
70) Overcoming Fear
71) Overcoming Prevailing Challenges
72) My life & Ministry
73) The Mystery of Praise

MIRACLE OF GOD MINISTRIES

NIGERIA CRUSADE 2012

MIRACLE OF GOD MINISTRIES
NIGERIA CRUSADE 2012

MIRACLE OF GOD MINISTRIES

NIGERIA CRUSADE

2012

MIRACLE OF GOD MINISTRIES

NIGERIA CRUSADE

2012

www.ingramcontent.com/pod-product-compliance
Lightning Source LLC
Chambersburg PA
CBHW022228010526
44113CB00033B/763